DO-IT-YOURSELF HOME

Canada

"Our Great Country"

Geography, History & Social Studies Handbook

By Ryan Conner, Serena Marie Lapointe
& Sarah Janisse Brown

Published By The Thinking Tree, LLC

WWW.FunschoolingBOOKS.com

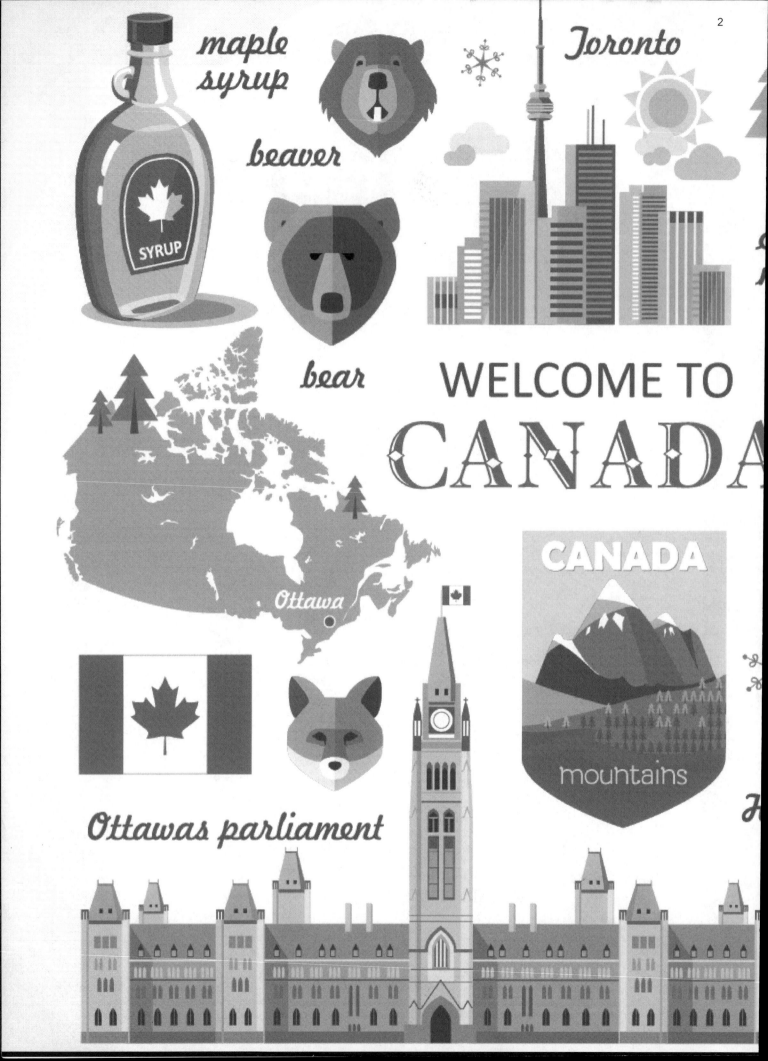

Do It Yourself Homeschooling

CANADA

Geography, History, and Social Studies Handbook

Name:

Date:

Contact Information:

About Me:

HOW TO USE THIS BOOK

This is a handbook for studying Canada's provinces and territories.

1. The provinces and territories are presented in alphabetical order.

2. You will use a variety of learning tools to research each province and territory.

LEARNING TOOLS REQUIRED TO COMPLETE THIS COURSE:

1. Library Books
2. A documentary or movie about each province or territory
3. Google Earth
4. Parent approved research websites such as Wikipedia.com
5. Canada atlas
6. Map of Canada
7. Colored pencils or gel pens
8. Black pens and #2 pencils for writing

This book can be used in order, or you can start with the province or territory of your choice!

ALL ABOUT CANADA

Draw the flag!

How did the flag come to be?

_____

_____

_____

_____

Where did the name "Canada" come from? From whom was it adopted?

_____

_____

_____

_____

_____

What year was the name adopted? Explain how different Canada was at the time.

_____

_____

_____

_____

Find and label:

Each province and territory

Each major body of water

Major cities (including the capital)

Mountain chains

Find and shade:

First Nation reserves in blue

French-speaking population in green

Uninhabited areas in red

List Canada's Prime Ministers

And The Years They Were In Office

1) _____

2) _____

3) _____

4) _____

5) _____

6) _____

7) _____

8) _____

9) _____

10) _____

11) _____

12) _____

13) _____

14) _____

15) _____

16) _____

17) _____

18) _____

19) _____

20) _____

21) _____

22) _____

23) _____

Draw three Prime Ministers here!

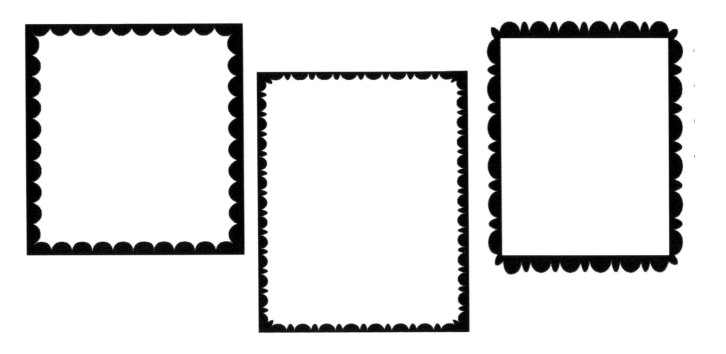

Write The National Anthem

_____

_____

_____

_____

_____

_____

_____

_____

_____

_____

_____

What does it mean to you?

_____

_____

_____

_____

Write down some of the funniest Canadian town names you can find!

Town name: Province or Territory:

_____   _____

_____   _____

_____   _____

_____   _____

_____   _____

_____   _____

_____   _____

OUR FIRST PEOPLES

What does "aboriginal" mean?

_____

_____

_____

Who are the First Nations people?

_____

_____

How long have they been in Canada?

_____

_____

For the purpose of study, historians grouped
"First Nations" peoples into six geographical areas.
List the groups:

_____

_____

_____

_____

_____

_____

Label and colour the groups on the map below.

OUR FIRST PEOPLES

Research and illustrate the homes and transportation that Canada's first peoples used.

Research and illustrate the tools, clothing, and food that Canada's first peoples used.

LIQUID GOLD

Canada is known for its delicious maple syrup.

Which province produces the most?

_____

How much does it produce?

_____

Research the indigenous history of
Canadian maple syrup.

_____
_____
_____
_____
_____
_____

Watch a video on sugar tapping and illustrate the process below.

CANADA'S FUR TRADE

Who were the voyageurs?

_____

_____

_____

What does "voyageur" mean?

_____

What is a portage?

_____

_____

_____

What goods did they transport?

_____

_____

_____

Where did they travel?

_____

_____

_____

Illustrate a voyageur canoe.

Illustrate the different goods
they transported.

CANADA HAS TWO NATIONAL SPORTS

What are they?

What years were they officially recognized?

Illustrate the two sports.

Canada has more lake area than any other country in the world!

List the 5 Great Lakes and illustrate a map of them.

_____

_____

_____

_____

_____

DINOSAURS!

Dinosaur Provincial Park is a UNESCO World Heritage site.

Where is it located?

_____

Why was it established?

_____

_____

_____

What are the badlands?

_____

_____

_____

List as many of the dinosaurs as you can.

_____

_____

_____

_____

_____

_____

Illustrate dinosaurs found in Dinosaur Provincial Park.

CANADA HAS TWO NATIONAL ANIMALS

What are they?

_____

What years were they chosen?

_____

Why were they chosen?

_____

Illustrate the two animals.

CANADA HAS TWO NATIONAL LANGUAGES

What are they?

_____

Choose 9 words in English and translate them into French.

English   French

_____   _____

_____   _____

_____   _____

_____   _____

_____   _____

_____   _____

_____   _____

_____   _____

_____   _____

PROVINCE STUDIES

ALBERTA

☐ Check this box once you've visited this province.

Find Alberta on this map and colour it in!

The capital of Alberta is _____

The population of Alberta is _____

The area of Alberta is _____

WRITE OR DRAW

Current Events	What to See
Draw the Flag	Famous Quote
Draw a Monument	Popular Exports

Find and label:

- The capital city and other major cities
- Important landmarks
- National parks
- Major highways and rivers
- Anything else you find interesting!

Draw and summarize an important historical event!

Draw a famous person from Alberta
or write a short biography about them!

Draw the official animal or write about it here.

Draw the official flower or write about it here.

Write a recipe for your favourite dish from Alberta!

Ingredients:

Preparation:

WATCH A MOVIE AND READ A BOOK THAT TAKES PLACE IN ALBERTA

Movie: Book:

Draw a scene from your movie!

Summarize a scene from your book!

WHAT DO YOU WANT TO DO IN ALBERTA?

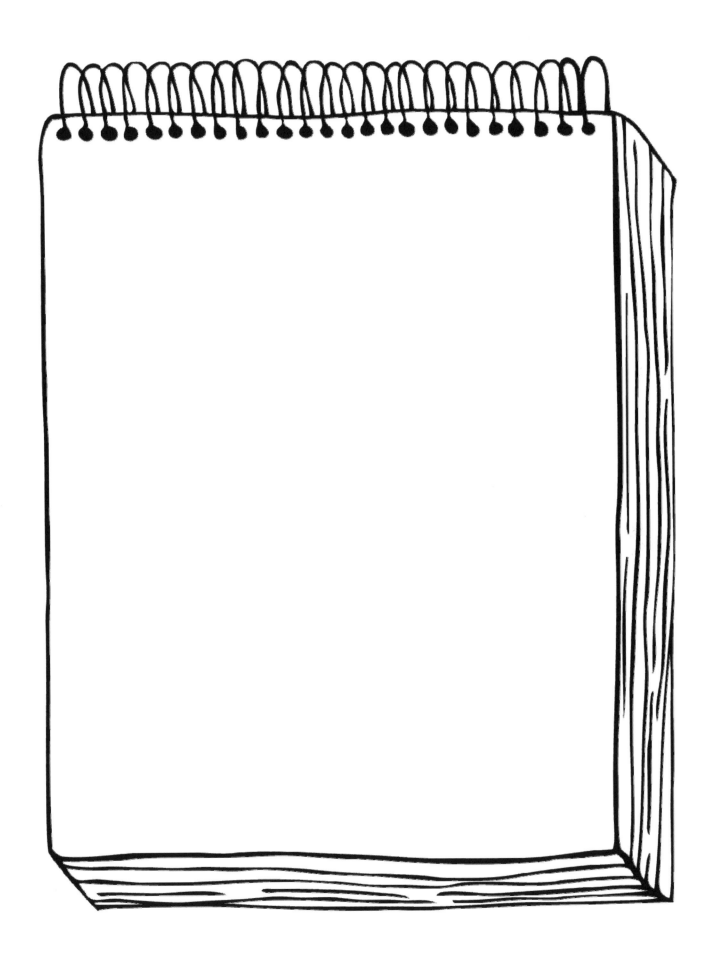

LIST 5 INTERESTING FACTS ABOUT ALBERTA

Illustrate your favourite!

CANADA WONDER SEARCH

A wonder is a fascinating place or thing.

Name of wonder: _____

List 5 interesting facts!

_____

_____

_____

_____

_____

Illustrate it!

BRITISH COLUMBIA

☐ Check this box once you've visited this province.

Find British Columbia on this map and colour it in!

The capital of British Columbia is _____

The population of British Columbia is _____

The area of British Columbia is _____

WRITE OR DRAW

Current Events	What to See
Draw the Flag	Famous Quote
Draw a Monument	Popular Exports

Find and label:

- The capital city and other major cities
- Important landmarks
- National parks
- Major highways and rivers
- Anything else you find interesting!

Draw and summarize an important historical event!

Draw a famous person from British Columbia
or write a short biography about them!

Draw the official
animal or write
about it here.

Draw the official
flower or write
about it here.

Write a recipe for your favourite dish from British Columbia!

Ingredients:

Preparation:

WATCH A MOVIE AND READ A BOOK THAT TAKES PLACE IN BRITISH COLUMBIA

Movie:

Book:

Draw a scene from your movie!

Summarize a scene from your book!

WHAT DO YOU WANT TO DO IN BRITISH COLUMBIA?

LIST 5 INTERESTING FACTS ABOUT BRITISH COLUMBIA

_____

_____

_____

_____

_____

Illustrate your favourite!

CANADA WONDER SEARCH

Name of wonder: _____

List 5 interesting facts!

_____

_____

_____

_____

_____

Illustrate it!

MANITOBA

☐ Check this box once you've visited this province.

Find on this map and colour it in!

The capital of Manitoba is _____

The population of Manitoba is _____

The area of Manitoba is _____

WRITE OR DRAW

Current Events	What to See
Draw the Flag	Famous Quote
Draw a Monument	Popular Exports

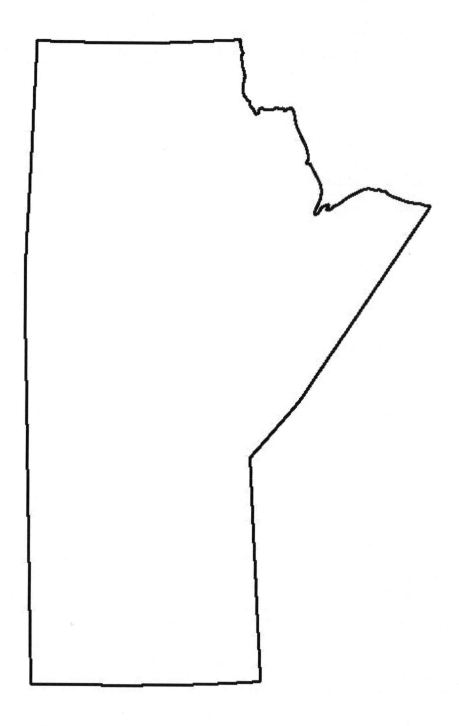

Find and label:

- The capital city and other major cities
- Important landmarks
- National parks
- Major highways and rivers
- Anything else you find interesting!

Draw and summarize an important historical event!

Draw a famous person from Manitoba
or write a short biography about them!

Draw the official
animal or write
about it here.

Draw the official
flower or write
about it here.

Write a recipe for your favourite dish from Manitoba!

Ingredients:

Preparation:

WATCH A MOVIE AND READ A BOOK THAT TAKES PLACE IN MANITOBA

Movie: Book:

Draw a scene from your movie!

Summarize a scene from your book!

WHAT DO YOU WANT TO DO IN MANITOBA?

LIST 5 INTERESTING FACTS ABOUT MANITOBA

Illustrate your favourite!

CANADA WONDER SEARCH

Name of wonder: _____

List 5 interesting facts!

_____

_____

_____

_____

_____

Illustrate it!

NEW BRUNSWICK

☐ Check this box once you've visited this province.

Find New Brunswick on this map and colour it in!

The capital of New Brunswick is _____

The population of New Brunswick is _____

The area of New Brunswick is _____

WRITE OR DRAW

Current Events	What to See
Draw the Flag	**Famous Quote**
Draw a Monument	**Popular Exports**

Find and label:

- The capital city and other major cities
- Important landmarks
- National parks
- Major highways and rivers
- Anything else you find interesting!

Draw and summarize an important historical event!

Draw a famous person from New Brunswick or write a short biography about them!

Draw the official animal or write about it here.

Draw the official flower or write about it here.

Write a recipe for your favourite dish from New Brunswick!

Ingredients:

Preparation:

_____

_____

_____

_____

_____

_____

_____

_____

_____

_____

_____

_____

WATCH A MOVIE AND READ A BOOK THAT TAKES PLACE IN NEW BRUNSWICK

Movie: Book:

Draw a scene from your movie!

Summarize a scene from your book!

WHAT DO YOU WANT TO DO IN NEW BRUNSWICK?

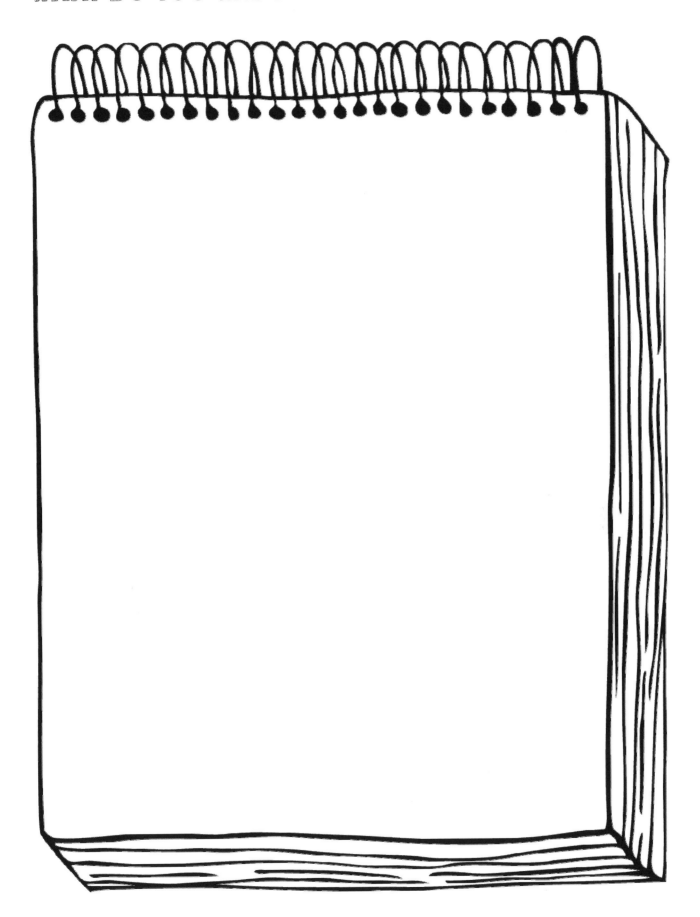

LIST 5 INTERESTING FACTS ABOUT NEW BRUNSWICK

_____

_____

_____

_____

_____

Illustrate your favourite!

CANADA WONDER SEARCH

Name of wonder: _____

List 5 interesting facts!

_____

_____

_____

_____

_____

Illustrate it!

NEWFOUNDLAND AND LABRADOR

☐ Check this box once you've visited this province.

Find NL on this map and colour it in!

The capital of NL is _____

The population of NL is _____

The area of NL is _____

WRITE OR DRAW

Current Events	What to See
Draw the Flag	**Famous Quote**
Draw a Monument	**Popular Exports**

Find and label:

- The capital city and other major cities

- Important landmarks

- National parks

- Major highways and rivers

- Anything else you find interesting!

Draw and summarize an important historical event!

Draw a famous person from Newfoundland and Labrador or write a short biography about them!

Draw the official animal or write about it here.

Draw the official flower or write about it here.

Write a recipe for your favourite dish from Newfoundland and Labrador!

Ingredients:

Preparation:

WATCH A MOVIE AND READ A BOOK THAT TAKES PLACE IN NL

Movie: Book:

Draw a scene from your movie!

Summarize a scene from your book!

WHAT DO YOU WANT TO DO IN NL?

LIST 5 INTERESTING FACTS ABOUT NEWFOUNDLAND AND LABRADOR

_____

_____

_____

_____

_____

Illustrate your favourite!

CANADA WONDER SEARCH

Name of wonder: _____

List 5 interesting facts!

_____

_____

_____

_____

_____

Illustrate it!

NORTHWEST TERRITORIES

☐ Check this box once you've visited this territory.

Find NWT on this map and colour it in!

The capital of NWT is _____

The population of NWT is _____

The area of NWT is _____

WRITE OR DRAW

Current Events	What to See
Draw the Flag	**Famous Quote**
Draw a Monument	**Popular Exports**

Find and label:

- The capital city and other major cities
- Important landmarks
- National parks
- Major highways and rivers
- Anything else you find interesting!

Draw and summarize an important historical event!

Draw a famous person from Northwest Territories or write a short biography about them!

Draw the official
animal or write
about it here.

Draw the official
flower or write
about it here.

Write a recipe for your favourite dish from Northwest Territories!

Ingredients:

Preparation:

_____

_____

_____

_____

_____

_____

_____

_____

_____

_____

_____

WATCH A MOVIE AND READ A BOOK THAT TAKES PLACE IN NWT

Movie: Book:

Draw a scene from your movie!

Summarize a scene from your book!

WHAT DO YOU WANT TO DO IN NWT?

LIST 5 INTERESTING FACTS ABOUT NORTHWEST TERRITORIES

_____

_____

_____

_____

_____

Illustrate your favourite!

CANADA WONDER SEARCH

Name of wonder: _____

List 5 interesting facts!

_____

_____

_____

_____

_____

Illustrate it!

NOVA SCOTIA

☐ Check this box once you've visited this province.

Find Nova Scotia on this map and colour it in!

The capital of Nova Scotia is _____

The population of Nova Scotia is _____

The area of Nova Scotia is _____

WRITE OR DRAW

Current Events	What to See
Draw the Flag	Famous Quote
Draw a Monument	Popular Exports

Find and label:

- The capital city and other major cities
- Important landmarks
- National parks
- Major highways and rivers
- Anything else you find interesting!

Draw and summarize an important historical event!

Draw a famous person from Nova Scotia
or write a short biography about them!

Draw the official
animal or write
about it here.

Draw the official
flower or write
about it here.

Write a recipe for your favourite dish from Nova Scotia!

Ingredients:

Preparation:

WATCH A MOVIE AND READ A BOOK THAT TAKES PLACE IN NOVA SCOTIA

Movie: Book:

Draw a scene from your movie!

Summarize a scene from your book!

WHAT DO YOU WANT TO DO IN NOVA SCOTIA?

LIST 5 INTERESTING FACTS ABOUT NOVA SCOTIA

_____

_____

_____

_____

_____

Illustrate your favourite!

CANADA WONDER SEARCH

Name of wonder: _____

List 5 interesting facts!

_____

_____

_____

_____

_____

Illustrate it!

NUNAVUT

☐ Check this box once you've visited this territory.

Find Nunavut on this map and colour it in!

The capital of Nunavut is _____

The population of Nunavut is _____

The area of Nunavut is _____

WRITE OR DRAW

Current Events	What to See
Draw the Flag	Famous Quote
Draw a Monument	Popular Exports

Find and label:

- The capital city and other major cities
- Important landmarks
- National parks
- Major highways and rivers
- Anything else you find interesting!

Draw and summarize an important historical event!

Draw a famous person from Nunavut
or write a short biography about them!

Draw the official animal or write about it here.

Draw the official flower or write about it here.

Write a recipe for your favourite dish from Nunavut!

Ingredients:

Preparation:

WATCH A MOVIE AND READ A BOOK THAT TAKES PLACE IN NUNAVUT

Movie: Book:

Draw a scene from your movie!

Summarize a scene from your book!

WHAT DO YOU WANT TO DO IN NUNAVUT?

LIST 5 INTERESTING FACTS ABOUT NUNAVUT

_____

_____

_____

_____

_____

Illustrate your favourite!

CANADA WONDER SEARCH

Name of wonder: _____

List 5 interesting facts!

_____

_____

_____

_____

_____

Illustrate it!

ONTARIO

☐ Check this box once you've visited this province.

Find Ontario on this map and colour it in!

The capital of Ontario is _____

The population of Ontario is _____

The area of Ontario is _____

WRITE OR DRAW

Current Events	What to See
Draw the Flag	Famous Quote
Draw a Monument	Popular Exports

Find and label:

- The capital city and other major cities

- Important landmarks

- National parks

- Major highways and rivers

- Anything else you find interesting!

Draw and summarize an important historical event!

Draw a famous person from Ontario
or write a short biography about them!

Draw the official animal or write about it here.

Draw the official flower or write about it here.

Write a recipe for your favourite dish from Ontario!

Ingredients:

Preparation:

WATCH A MOVIE AND READ A BOOK THAT TAKES PLACE IN ONTARIO

Movie: Book:

Draw a scene from your movie!

Summarize a scene from your book!

WHAT DO YOU WANT TO DO IN ONTARIO?

LIST 5 INTERESTING FACTS ABOUT ONTARIO

_____

_____

_____

_____

_____

Illustrate your favourite!

CANADA WONDER SEARCH

Name of wonder: _____

List 5 interesting facts!

_____

_____

_____

_____

_____

Illustrate it!

PRINCE EDWARD ISLAND

☐ Check this box once you've visited this province.

Find PEI on this map and colour it in!

The capital of PEI is _____

The population of PEI is _____

The area of PEI is _____

WRITE OR DRAW

Current Events	What to See
Draw the Flag	**Famous Quote**
Draw a Monument	**Popular Exports**

Find and label:

- The capital city and other major cities

- Important landmarks

- National parks

- Major highways and rivers

- Anything else you find interesting!

Draw and summarize an important historical event!

Draw a famous person from PEI
or write a short biography about them!

Draw the official animal or write about it here.

Draw the official flower or write about it here.

Write a recipe for your favourite dish from Prince Edward Island!

Ingredients:

Preparation:

WATCH A MOVIE AND READ A BOOK THAT TAKES PLACE IN PEI

Movie: Book:

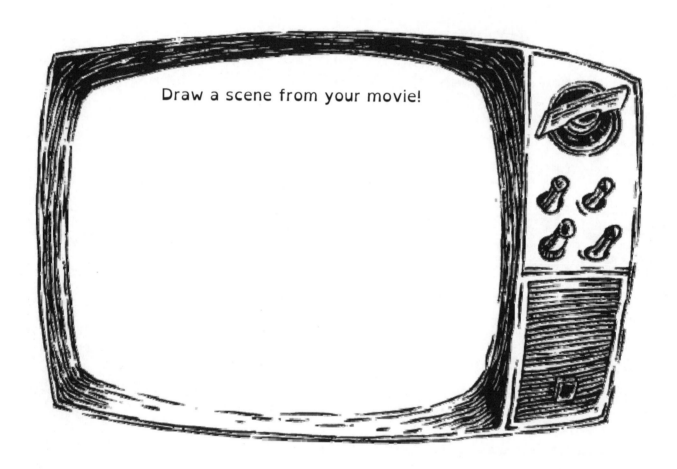

Draw a scene from your movie!

Summarize a scene from your book!

WHAT DO YOU WANT TO DO IN PEI?

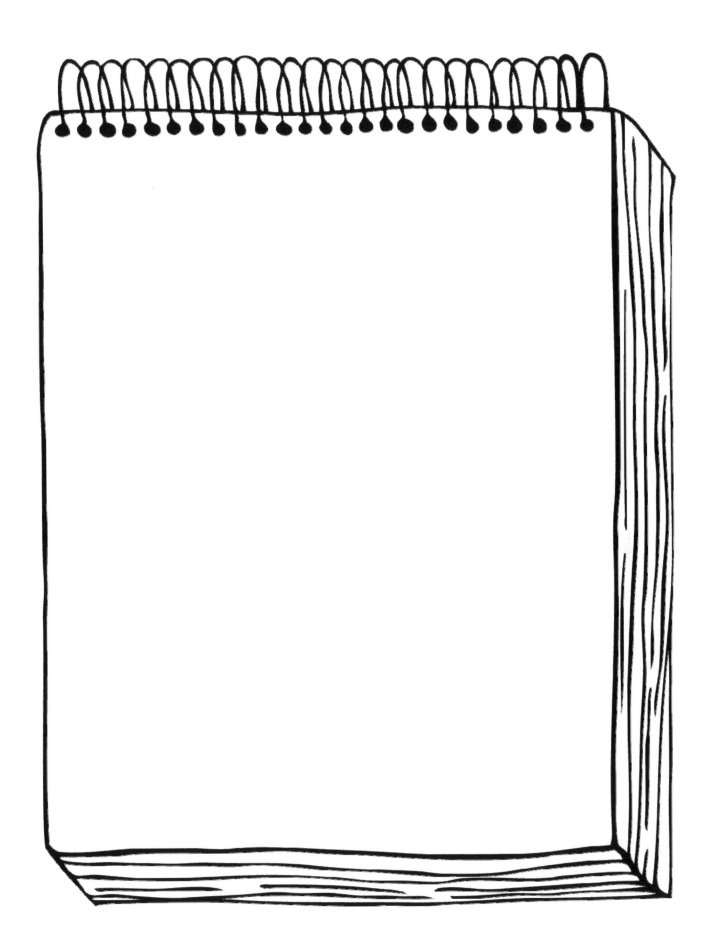

LIST 5 INTERESTING FACTS ABOUT PRINCE EDWARD ISLAND

_____

_____

_____

_____

_____

Illustrate your favourite!

CANADA WONDER SEARCH

Name of wonder: _____

List 5 interesting facts!

_____

_____

_____

_____

_____

Illustrate it!

QUEBEC

☐ Check this box once you've visited this province.

Find Quebec on this map and colour it in!

The capital of Quebec is _____

The population of Quebec is _____

The area of Quebec is _____

WRITE OR DRAW

Current Events	What to See

Draw the Flag	Famous Quote

Draw a Monument	Popular Exports

Find and label:

- The capital city and other major cities

- Important landmarks

- National parks

- Major highways and rivers

- Anything else you find interesting!

Draw and summarize an important historical event!

Draw a famous person from Quebec
or write a short biography about them!

Draw the official animal or write about it here.

Draw the official flower or write about it here.

Write a recipe for your favourite dish from Quebec!

Ingredients:

Preparation:
_____

_____

_____

_____

_____

_____

_____

_____

_____

_____

_____

WATCH A MOVIE AND READ A BOOK THAT TAKES PLACE IN QUEBEC

Movie:

Book:

Draw a scene from your movie!

Summarize a scene from your book!

WHAT DO YOU WANT TO DO IN QUEBEC?

LIST 5 INTERESTING FACTS ABOUT QUEBEC

_____

_____

_____

_____

_____

Illustrate your favourite!

CANADA WONDER SEARCH

Name of wonder: _____

List 5 interesting facts!

_____

_____

_____

_____

_____

Illustrate it!

SASKATCHEWAN

☐ Check this box once you've visited this province.

Find Saskatchewan on this map and colour it in!

The capital of Saskatchewan is _____

The population of Saskatchewan is _____

The area of Saskatchewan is _____

WRITE OR DRAW

Current Events	What to See

Draw the Flag	Famous Quote

Draw a Monument	Popular Exports

Find and label:

- The capital city and other major cities
- Important landmarks
- National parks
- Major highways and rivers
- Anything else you find interesting!

Draw and summarize an important historical event!

Draw a famous person from Saskatchewan
or write a short biography about them!

166

Draw the official
animal or write
about it here.

Draw the official
flower or write
about it here.

Write a recipe for your favourite dish from Saskatchewan!

Ingredients:

Preparation:

WATCH A MOVIE AND READ A BOOK THAT TAKES PLACE IN SASKATCHEWAN

Movie: Book:

Draw a scene from your movie!

Summarize a scene from your book!

WHAT DO YOU WANT TO DO IN SASKATCHEWAN?

LIST 5 INTERESTING FACTS ABOUT SASKATCHEWAN

_____

_____

_____

_____

_____

Illustrate your favourite!

CANADA WONDER SEARCH

Name of wonder: _____

List 5 interesting facts!

_____

_____

_____

_____

_____

Illustrate it!

YUKON

Check this box once you've visited this territory.

Find Yukon on this map and colour it in!

The capital of Yukon is _____

The population of Yukon is _____

The area of Yukon is _____

WRITE OR DRAW

Current Events	What to See
Draw the Flag	Famous Quote
Draw a Monument	Popular Exports

Find and label:

- The capital city and other major cities

- Important landmarks

- National parks

- Major highways and rivers

- Anything else you find interesting!

Draw and summarize an important historical event!

Draw a famous person from Yukon or write a short biography about them!

Draw the official
animal or write
about it here.

Draw the official
flower or write
about it here.

Write a recipe for your favourite dish from Yukon!

Ingredients:

Preparation:

WATCH A MOVIE AND READ A BOOK THAT TAKES PLACE IN YUKON

Movie: Book:

Draw a scene from your movie!

Summarize a scene from your book!

WHAT DO YOU WANT TO DO IN YUKON?

LIST 5 INTERESTING FACTS ABOUT YUKON

Illustrate your favourite!

CANADA WONDER SEARCH

Name of wonder: _____

List 5 interesting facts!

_____

_____

_____

_____

_____

Illustrate it!

CANADIAN
INVENTION SEARCH

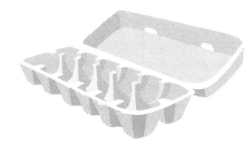

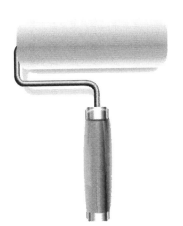

CANADIAN
INVENTION SEARCH

Name of invention:

Name of inventor:

What year was it invented?

Purpose of invention:

Illustrate it!

CANADIAN
INVENTION SEARCH

Name of invention:

Name of inventor:

What year was it invented?

Purpose of invention:

Illustrate it!

CANADIAN INVENTION SEARCH

Name of invention:

Name of inventor:

What year was it invented?

Purpose of invention:

Illustrate it!

CANADIAN
INVENTION SEARCH

Name of invention:

Name of inventor:

What year was it invented?

Purpose of invention:

Illustrate it!

CANADIAN INVENTION SEARCH

Name of invention:

Name of inventor:

What year was it invented?

Purpose of invention:

Illustrate it!

CANADIAN
INVENTION SEARCH

Name of invention:

Name of inventor:

What year was it invented?

Purpose of invention:

Illustrate it!

This Bundle includes:

Devotional Homeschool Journal for Christian Girls
50 Creative Writing Prompts
Just for Teen Girls Bible Study Journal
The Singer and the Songwriter
The Singer & the Songwriter Companion Book
Book of Cultures & Communities
Are You a Math Genius

Dyslexia Games Series C (8 Books)

thethinkingtreebranch.com/fpea-convention-specials

Thinking Tree Bundle

LEVEL C
JUST FOR CREATIVE
TEEN GIRLS
High School
Ideal for Ages 13+

This Bundle includes:

Teen Guys Journal (Core Journal)
Science Handbook & Portfolio
Timeline of World History
Master Class
Math Genius
50 Creative Writing Prompts
Dyslexia Games Series C (8 Books)

thethinkingtreebranch.com/fpea-convention-specials

Thinking Tree Bundle

LEVEL C
JUST FOR
TEEN GUYS
High School
Ideal for Ages 13+

The Thinking Tree, LLC

Copyright Information:

Made in the USA
Columbia, SC
23 February 2020